The All American Cookbook

The American Pantry Collection™

Published by:
Apricot Press, Inc.
Box 1611
American Fork, Utah
84003

books@apricotpress.com
www.apricotpress.com

ISBN 1-885027-15-X

Cover Design & Layout by David Mecham
Printed in the United States of America

Forward

Not long ago I was sitting in a popular Mexican restaurant enjoying a terrific meal, when a Hispanic gentleman paused at my table and gently quipped in a thick accent, "This is not REAL Mexican food."

The idea of a melting pot is as American as it gets. If you were to ask most people to name their favorite American recipes, if you looked closely, you would see that most dishes have been imported from some other country. However, if you looked again, you might also observe that the recipe's roots had come from another country, but much like her citizens, after staying in this country for a while, the American version of this food would have changed from the original; it would have evolved until it had become clearly American.

In this book we have tried to convey in food and thought, the essence of America. We have shared with you the recipes, which we think you will enjoy. And we have shared quotes which flavor the food with attitudes and thoughts that are also clearly "American," to create an exclusively American ambiance. We sincerely hope you enjoy the feast. Dig in!

E.W. Allred

This book is dedicated to all those who
have laid down their lives, and who would
willingly lay down their lives today if necessary
so that this great government of the people,
by the people, and for the people will not end,
so future generations can enjoy the liberty,
the prosperity, and the peace,
which can only come to a free people.

RECIPES

As American As Apple Pie
APPLE PIE

6 to 8 apples (McIntosh are favorites) peeled and sliced to make 7 cups*

1 cup sugar

1/4 teaspoon salt

2 tablespoons flour

1 teaspoon cinnamon

1/4 teaspoon nutmeg

2 tablespoons butter or margarine

9 inch pie-pastry shell

Directions:

1. Mix sugar, salt, flour, and spices with apples.
2. Fill pie shell with mixture.
3. Place slices or pats of butter on top.
4. Place top crust and seal.
5. Use knife to poke holes in crust so steam can escape or crisscross top crust.
6. Sprinkle top with sugar and cinnamon.
7. Bake at 400 degrees for 50 minutes or until done.
8. Slice and serve warm or with a scoop of vanilla ice cream.

* If substituting canned-pie-sliced apples in liquid or pineapple, use 2 4-ounce cans or 5-1/2 cups drained.

"Give us your tired, your poor, your huddled masses yearning to breath free; send these, the homeless tempest tossed to me....I lift my lamp beside the golden door..."

**Inscription on the Statue of Liberty,
New York Harbor**

"More die in the United States from too much food than from too little."

John Kenneth Galbraith

"The government is best which governs least."

Henry David Thoreau, 1849

As American As
APPLE PUDDING

1 cup sugar	1 teaspoon cinnamon
1/2 square margarine	1/4 teaspoon nutmeg
1 egg	1/2 teaspoon salt
2 cups grated apples	1/2 teaspoon vanilla
1/2 cup chopped nuts	1 cup flour
1 teaspoon soda	

Directions:

1. Stir sugar and margarine together into creamy texture.
2. Add the egg and beat.
3. Add apples, flour, cinnamon, nutmeg, salt, soda, and vanilla and stir.
4. Add chopped nuts.
5. Bake in greased pan at 350 degrees for 45 minutes.
6. Serve warm and top with whipped cream or caramel sauce.

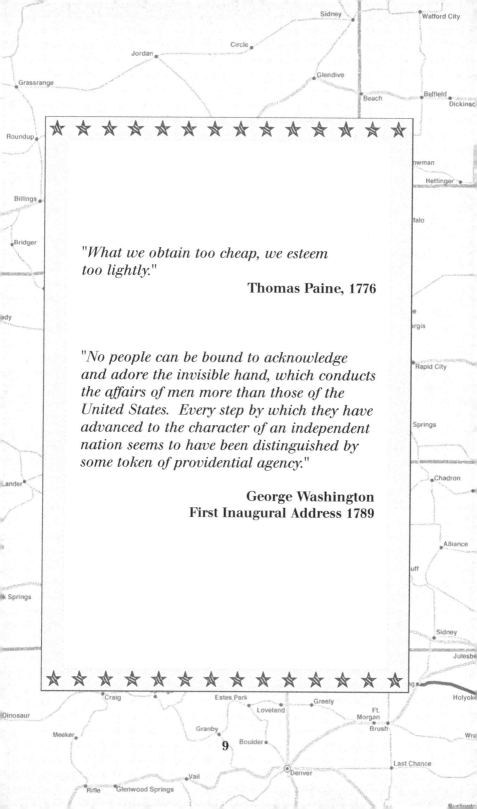

"What we obtain too cheap, we esteem too lightly."

Thomas Paine, 1776

"No people can be bound to acknowledge and adore the invisible hand, which conducts the affairs of men more than those of the United States. Every step by which they have advanced to the character of an independent nation seems to have been distinguished by some token of providential agency."

**George Washington
First Inaugural Address 1789**

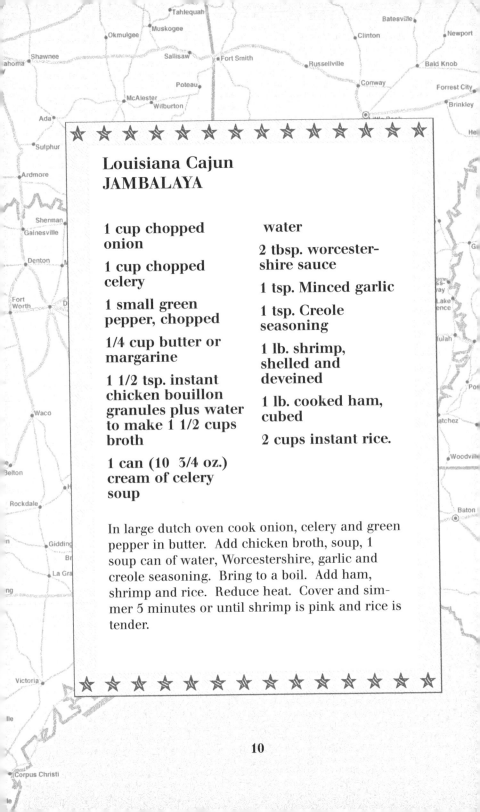

Louisiana Cajun
JAMBALAYA

1 cup chopped onion

1 cup chopped celery

1 small green pepper, chopped

1/4 cup butter or margarine

1 1/2 tsp. instant chicken bouillon granules plus water to make 1 1/2 cups broth

1 can (10 3/4 oz.) cream of celery soup

water

2 tbsp. worcestershire sauce

1 tsp. Minced garlic

1 tsp. Creole seasoning

1 lb. shrimp, shelled and deveined

1 lb. cooked ham, cubed

2 cups instant rice.

In large dutch oven cook onion, celery and green pepper in butter. Add chicken broth, soup, 1 soup can of water, Worcestershire, garlic and creole seasoning. Bring to a boil. Add ham, shrimp and rice. Reduce heat. Cover and simmer 5 minutes or until shrimp is pink and rice is tender.

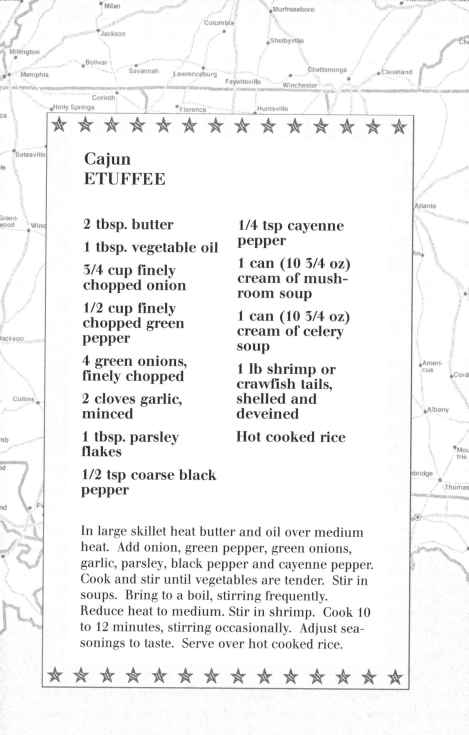

Cajun
ETUFFEE

2 tbsp. butter

1 tbsp. vegetable oil

3/4 cup finely chopped onion

1/2 cup finely chopped green pepper

4 green onions, finely chopped

2 cloves garlic, minced

1 tbsp. parsley flakes

1/2 tsp coarse black pepper

1/4 tsp cayenne pepper

1 can (10 3/4 oz) cream of mushroom soup

1 can (10 3/4 oz) cream of celery soup

1 lb shrimp or crawfish tails, shelled and deveined

Hot cooked rice

In large skillet heat butter and oil over medium heat. Add onion, green pepper, green onions, garlic, parsley, black pepper and cayenne pepper. Cook and stir until vegetables are tender. Stir in soups. Bring to a boil, stirring frequently. Reduce heat to medium. Stir in shrimp. Cook 10 to 12 minutes, stirring occasionally. Adjust seasonings to taste. Serve over hot cooked rice.

11

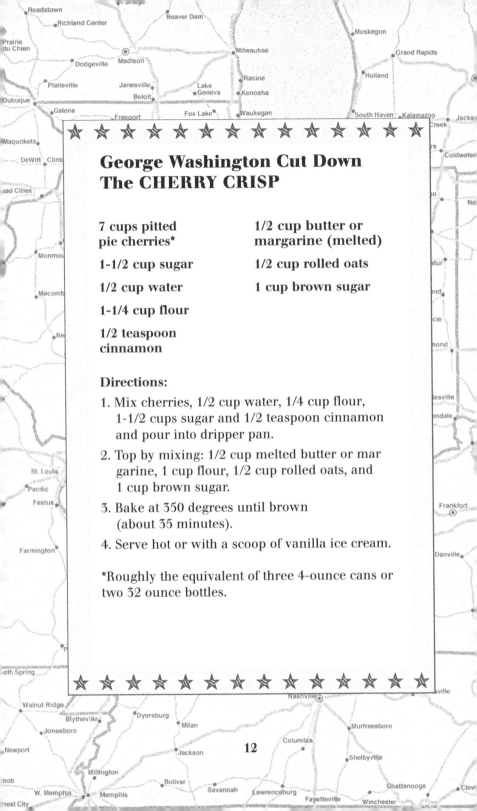

George Washington Cut Down The CHERRY CRISP

7 cups pitted pie cherries*	1/2 cup butter or margarine (melted)
1-1/2 cup sugar	1/2 cup rolled oats
1/2 cup water	1 cup brown sugar
1-1/4 cup flour	
1/2 teaspoon cinnamon	

Directions:

1. Mix cherries, 1/2 cup water, 1/4 cup flour, 1-1/2 cups sugar and 1/2 teaspoon cinnamon and pour into dripper pan.

2. Top by mixing: 1/2 cup melted butter or margarine, 1 cup flour, 1/2 cup rolled oats, and 1 cup brown sugar.

3. Bake at 350 degrees until brown (about 35 minutes).

4. Serve hot or with a scoop of vanilla ice cream.

*Roughly the equivalent of three 4-ounce cans or two 32 ounce bottles.

"We must all hang together, or we will all most certainly hang separately."

**Benjamin Franklin
commenting at the signing
of the Declaration of Independence.**

"The path we have chosen for the present is full of hazards...the cost of freedom is always high, but Americans have always paid it. And one path we shall never choose, and that is the path of surrender or submission."

**John F. Kennedy
while announcing the blockade of Cuba at
the height of the Cuban missile crisis
Oct. 22, 1962**

"The Revolution was affected before the war commenced. The Revolution was in the minds and hearts of the people."

**John Adams
1818**

13

Squanto's Thanksgiving
PUMPKIN PIE

1-1/2 cups canned pumpkin

3/4 cup sugar

1/2 teaspoon salt

1/4 teaspoon ground cloves

1/4 teaspoon ground nutmeg

1 teaspoon ground cinnamon

3/4 teaspoon ground ginger

3 eggs

2/3 cup evaporated milk

1-1/4 cup milk

Instructions:

1. Mix all the ingredients with pumpkin.

2. Fold until well-mixed and texture is uniform.

3. Pour into 9-inch pie shell.

4. Bake at 400 degrees for 50 minutes. You can be certain the pie is properly done if you insert a knife blade into the middle of the pie. If the blade comes out clean, the pie is done.

5. Cool, cut, and serve with whipped cream on top.

"These are the times that try men's souls. The summer soldier and the sunshine patriot will, in this crisis, shrink from the service of their country; but he that stands it now, deserves the love and thanks of man and woman."

Thomas Paine
December 1776

"Timid men...prefer the calm of despotism to the boisterous sea of liberty."

Thomas Jefferson
1796

15

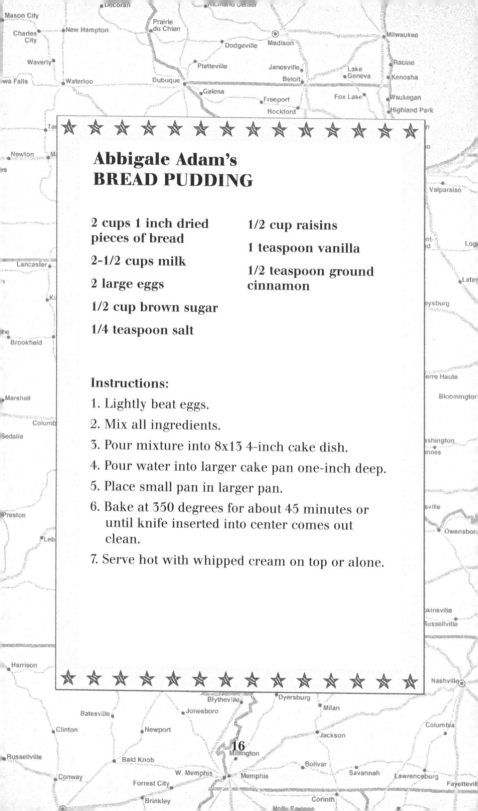

Abbigale Adam's
BREAD PUDDING

2 cups 1 inch dried pieces of bread

2-1/2 cups milk

2 large eggs

1/2 cup brown sugar

1/4 teaspoon salt

1/2 cup raisins

1 teaspoon vanilla

1/2 teaspoon ground cinnamon

Instructions:

1. Lightly beat eggs.
2. Mix all ingredients.
3. Pour mixture into 8x13 4-inch cake dish.
4. Pour water into larger cake pan one-inch deep.
5. Place small pan in larger pan.
6. Bake at 350 degrees for about 45 minutes or until knife inserted into center comes out clean.
7. Serve hot with whipped cream on top or alone.

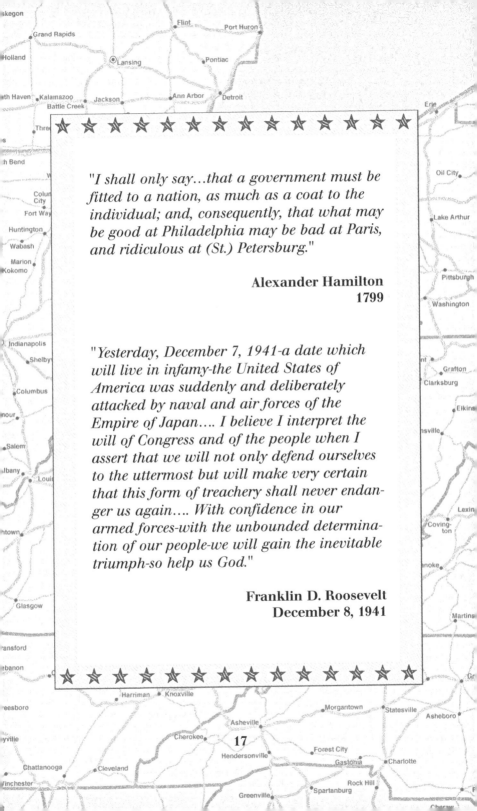

"*I shall only say…that a government must be fitted to a nation, as much as a coat to the individual; and, consequently, that what may be good at Philadelphia may be bad at Paris, and ridiculous at (St.) Petersburg.*"

Alexander Hamilton
1799

"*Yesterday, December 7, 1941-a date which will live in infamy-the United States of America was suddenly and deliberately attacked by naval and air forces of the Empire of Japan…. I believe I interpret the will of Congress and of the people when I assert that we will not only defend ourselves to the uttermost but will make very certain that this form of treachery shall never endanger us again…. With confidence in our armed forces-with the unbounded determination of our people-we will gain the inevitable triumph-so help us God.*"

Franklin D. Roosevelt
December 8, 1941

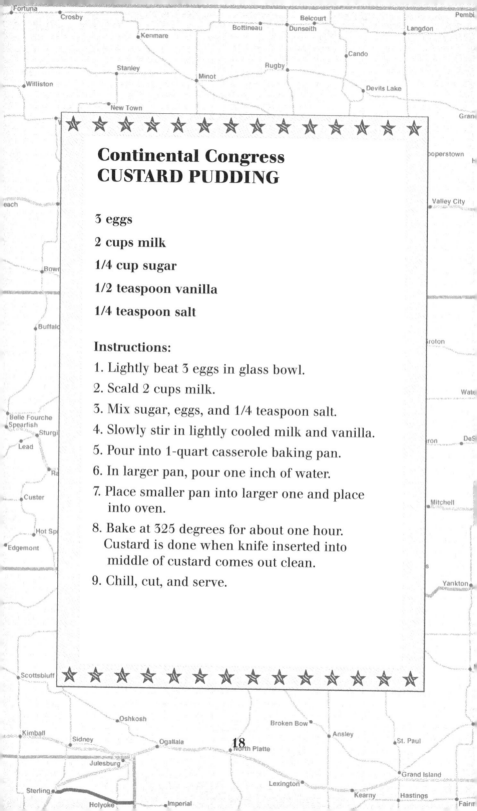

Continental Congress
CUSTARD PUDDING

3 eggs

2 cups milk

1/4 cup sugar

1/2 teaspoon vanilla

1/4 teaspoon salt

Instructions:

1. Lightly beat 3 eggs in glass bowl.
2. Scald 2 cups milk.
3. Mix sugar, eggs, and 1/4 teaspoon salt.
4. Slowly stir in lightly cooled milk and vanilla.
5. Pour into 1-quart casserole baking pan.
6. In larger pan, pour one inch of water.
7. Place smaller pan into larger one and place into oven.
8. Bake at 325 degrees for about one hour. Custard is done when knife inserted into middle of custard comes out clean.
9. Chill, cut, and serve.

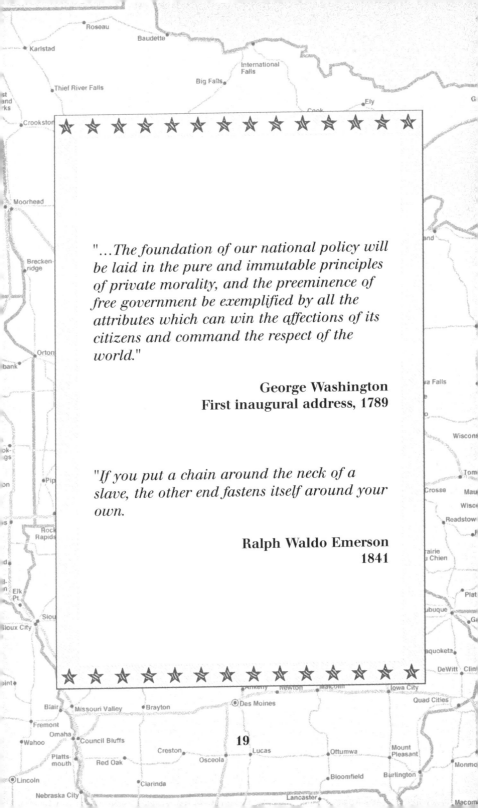

"...*The foundation of our national policy will be laid in the pure and immutable principles of private morality, and the preeminence of free government be exemplified by all the attributes which can win the affections of its citizens and command the respect of the world.*"

George Washington
First inaugural address, 1789

"*If you put a chain around the neck of a slave, the other end fastens itself around your own.*

Ralph Waldo Emerson
1841

19

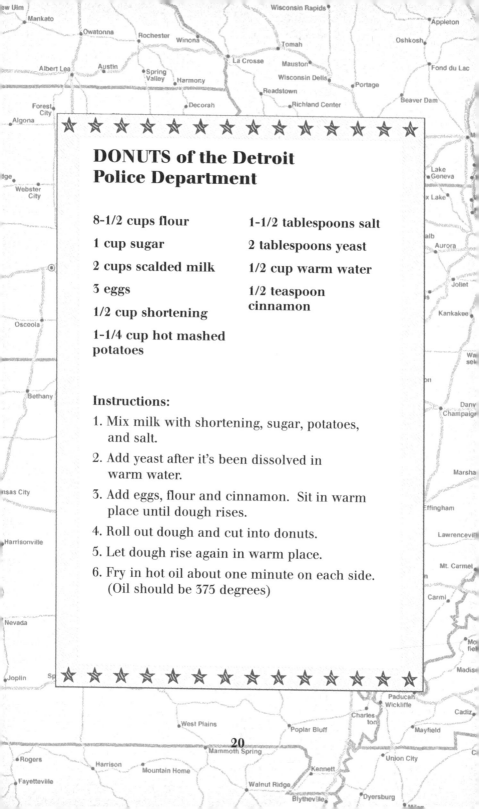

DONUTS of the Detroit Police Department

8-1/2 cups flour	1-1/2 tablespoons salt
1 cup sugar	2 tablespoons yeast
2 cups scalded milk	1/2 cup warm water
3 eggs	1/2 teaspoon cinnamon
1/2 cup shortening	
1-1/4 cup hot mashed potatoes	

Instructions:

1. Mix milk with shortening, sugar, potatoes, and salt.
2. Add yeast after it's been dissolved in warm water.
3. Add eggs, flour and cinnamon. Sit in warm place until dough rises.
4. Roll out dough and cut into donuts.
5. Let dough rise again in warm place.
6. Fry in hot oil about one minute on each side. (Oil should be 375 degrees)

"This was the first nation in the history of the world to be founded with a purpose. The great phrases of that purpose still sound in every American heart, North and South: 'All men are created equal'-'government by the consent of the governed....' Well, those are not just clever words, or those are not just empty theories. In their name Americans have fought and died for two centuries...."

**Lindon Baines Johnson
1965**

"As a nation we may take pride in the fact that we are soft hearted; but we cannot afford to be soft-headed."

**Franklin D. Roosevelt
1941**

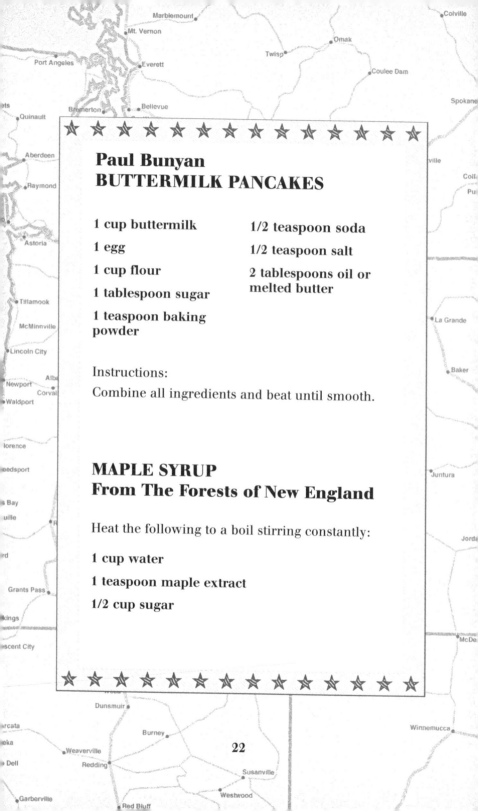

Paul Bunyan
BUTTERMILK PANCAKES

1 cup buttermilk

1 egg

1 cup flour

1 tablespoon sugar

1 teaspoon baking powder

1/2 teaspoon soda

1/2 teaspoon salt

2 tablespoons oil or melted butter

Instructions:

Combine all ingredients and beat until smooth.

MAPLE SYRUP
From The Forests of New England

Heat the following to a boil stirring constantly:

1 cup water

1 teaspoon maple extract

1/2 cup sugar

"Fourscore and seven years ago our fathers brought forth on this continent a new nation, conceived in liberty, and dedicated to the proposition that all men are created equal.

Now we are engaged in a great civil war, testing whether that nation, or any nation so conceived and so dedicated, can long endure. We are met on a great battlefield of that war. We have come to dedicate a portion of that field as a final resting-place for those who here gave their lives that that nation might live. It is altogether fitting and proper that we should do this.

But, in a larger sense, we cannot dedicate-we cannot consecrate-we cannot hallow-this ground. The brave men, living and dead, who struggled here, have consecrated it far above our poor power to add or detract. The world will little note nor long remember what we say here, but it can never forget what they did here. It is for us, the living, rather, to be dedicated here to the unfinished work, which they who fought here have thus far so nobly advanced. It is rather for us to be here dedicated to the great task remaining before us-that from these honored dead we take increased devotion to that cause for which they gave last full measure of devotion; that we here highly resolve that these dead shall not have died in vain; that this nation, under God, shall have a new birth of freedom; and that government of the people, by the people, for the people, shall not perish from the earth.

Abraham Lincoln

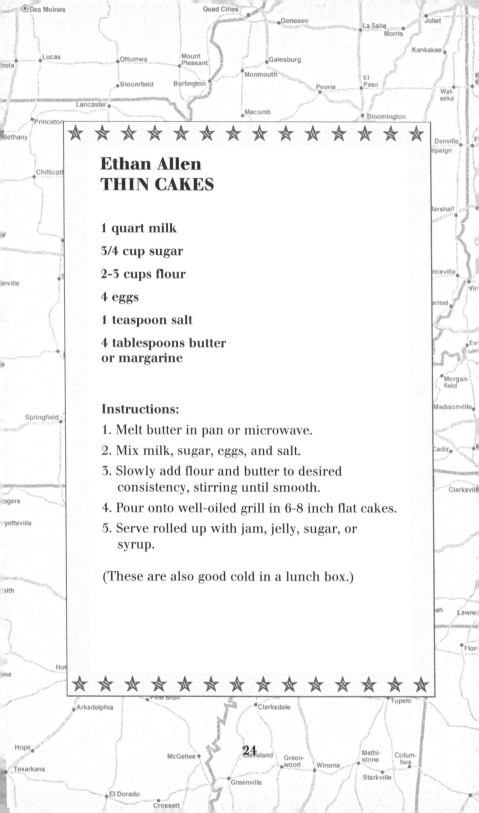

Ethan Allen
THIN CAKES

1 quart milk

3/4 cup sugar

2-3 cups flour

4 eggs

1 teaspoon salt

4 tablespoons butter
or margarine

Instructions:

1. Melt butter in pan or microwave.
2. Mix milk, sugar, eggs, and salt.
3. Slowly add flour and butter to desired
   consistency, stirring until smooth.
4. Pour onto well-oiled grill in 6-8 inch flat cakes.
5. Serve rolled up with jam, jelly, sugar, or
   syrup.

(These are also good cold in a lunch box.)

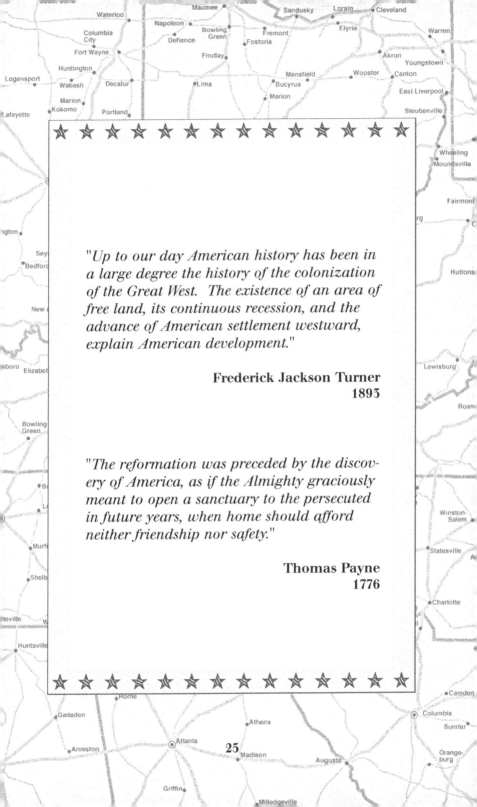

"*Up to our day American history has been in a large degree the history of the colonization of the Great West. The existence of an area of free land, its continuous recession, and the advance of American settlement westward, explain American development.*"

Frederick Jackson Turner
1893

"*The reformation was preceded by the discovery of America, as if the Almighty graciously meant to open a sanctuary to the persecuted in future years, when home should afford neither friendship nor safety.*"

Thomas Payne
1776

25

Cooking The
THANKSGIVING TURKEY

When buying the turkey, plan for 1/2 to 3/4 pounds
per person you plan to serve. Make certain turkey
is thawed according to the instructions on the
package. Since stuffing will expand during cooking,
do not pack stuffing tightly into cavity. Fold wings
across turkeys back with tips touching, and then fill
body cavity with stuffing (if desired). Tie drum-
sticks together with heavy string, then tie to tail.

Preheat oven to 325 degrees. Place turkey breast up
on rack in shallow roasting pan. Brush with butter.
Insert meat thermometer so tip is in the thickest
part of breast meat and does not touch bone. When
turkey skin begins to turn golden, loosely place tent
of aluminum foil over bird. When the turkey is 2/3
done, cut string holding legs.

Cooking Timetable:

6 to 8 pounds	3 to 3-1/2 hours
8 to 12 pounds	3-1/2 to 4-1/2 hours
12 to 16 pounds	4-1/2 to 5-1/2 hours
16 to 20 pounds	5-1/2 to 6-1/2 hours
20 to 24 pounds	6-1/2 to 7 hours

When turkey is done, drumstick meat should be
very soft.

*Internal temperature should be 185 degrees.
**Times will be slightly less for unstuffed turkeys

" *In democracy, the individual enjoys not only the ultimate power but carries the ultimate responsibility.*"

Norman Cousins

"*We cannot always assure the future of our friends; we have a better chance of assuring our future if we remember who our friends are.*"

Henry Kissinger

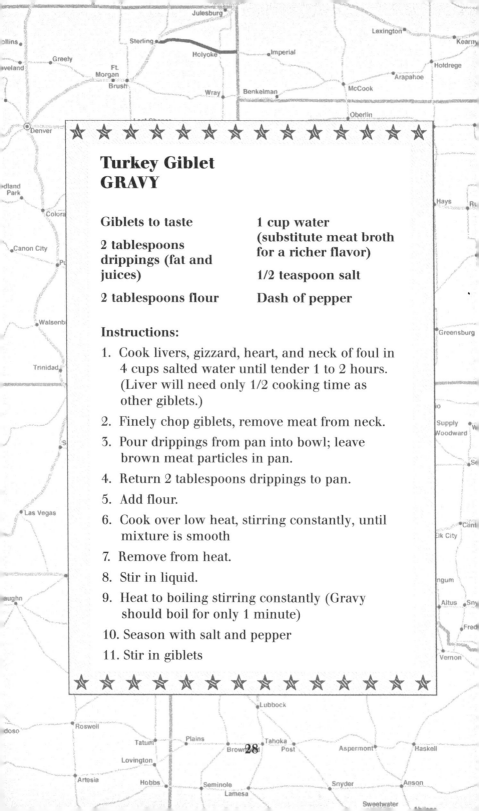

Turkey Giblet GRAVY

Giblets to taste

2 tablespoons drippings (fat and juices)

2 tablespoons flour

1 cup water (substitute meat broth for a richer flavor)

1/2 teaspoon salt

Dash of pepper

Instructions:

1. Cook livers, gizzard, heart, and neck of foul in 4 cups salted water until tender 1 to 2 hours. (Liver will need only 1/2 cooking time as other giblets.)
2. Finely chop giblets, remove meat from neck.
3. Pour drippings from pan into bowl; leave brown meat particles in pan.
4. Return 2 tablespoons drippings to pan.
5. Add flour.
6. Cook over low heat, stirring constantly, until mixture is smooth
7. Remove from heat.
8. Stir in liquid.
9. Heat to boiling stirring constantly (Gravy should boil for only 1 minute)
10. Season with salt and pepper
11. Stir in giblets

"*The government is us; we are the government, you and I.*"

Theodore Roosevelt

"*The right of the people to be secure in their persons, houses, papers, and effects, against unreasonable searches and seizures, shall not be violated, and no warrants shall issue but upon probable cause, supported by oath or affirmation, and particularly describing the place to be searched, and the persons or things to be seized.*"

Bill of Rights
4th Amendment to the Constitution

"*Let us resolve to be masters, not the victims, of our history, controlling our own destiny without giving way to blind suspicions and emotions.*"

John F. Kennedy

Wisconsin
CHEESY POTATO CORN SOUP

1/4 cup chopped onion

1/4 cup shopped red sweet pepper

1/2 cup finely chopped celery

1 tbsp. olive oil

2 cups diced potatoes

1 can (14.5 oz.) chicken broth

2 cans (15 oz. each) whole kernel sweet corn

3 cups milk

1/2 cup shredded process American cheese (2 oz.)

salt

black pepper

In large saucepan cook onion, red pepper and celery in oil 3 minutes or until tender. Add potatoes and broth. Bring to a boil; reduce heat. Cover and simmer 8 to 10 minutes or until potatoes are tender. Add corn, milk and cheese. Cook and stir until heated through and cheese is melted. Season to taste with salt and pepper.

Georgia Peach
PIZZA

1 pouch Sugar
Cookie Mix

1 Can (15 oz)
Raspberry flavor
sliced peaches

2 8 oz pkg. cream
cheese, softened

1/3 cup sugar

1/2 tsp. almond
extract

fresh raspberries,
blueberries and/or
halved strawberries

Prepare cookie mix as directed on package. Roll
dough into 12-inch circle. Place dough on 12-
inch pizza pan. Bake as directed. Cool.
Meanwhile, drain peaches, preserving 1/3 cup
syrup. For filling, in bowl stir together cream
cheese, sugar, almond extract and the 1/3 cup
reserved syrup until creamy; refrigerate. Spread
filling over cooled crust. Arrange peach slices
and berries on filling. Cover and chill 2 to 24
hours. Serve with whipped dessert topping, if
desired. Garnish with fresh mint, if desired.
Store any leftover pizza in refrigerator.

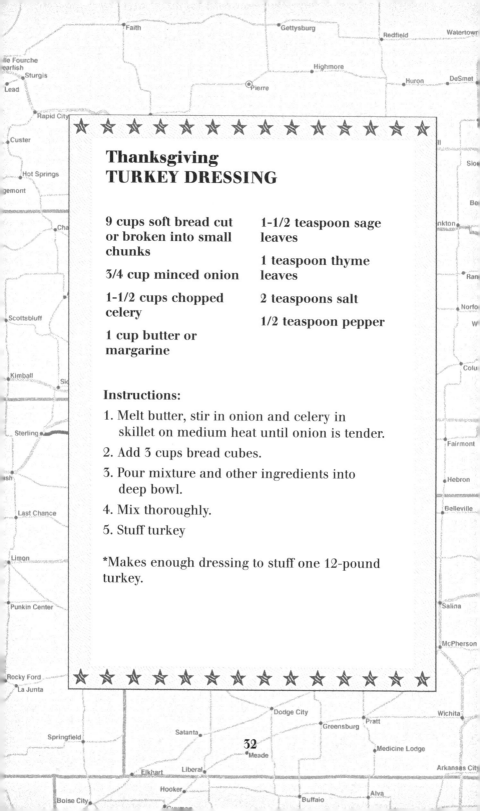

Thanksgiving
TURKEY DRESSING

9 cups soft bread cut or broken into small chunks

3/4 cup minced onion

1-1/2 cups chopped celery

1 cup butter or margarine

1-1/2 teaspoon sage leaves

1 teaspoon thyme leaves

2 teaspoons salt

1/2 teaspoon pepper

Instructions:

1. Melt butter, stir in onion and celery in skillet on medium heat until onion is tender.

2. Add 3 cups bread cubes.

3. Pour mixture and other ingredients into deep bowl.

4. Mix thoroughly.

5. Stuff turkey

*Makes enough dressing to stuff one 12-pound turkey.

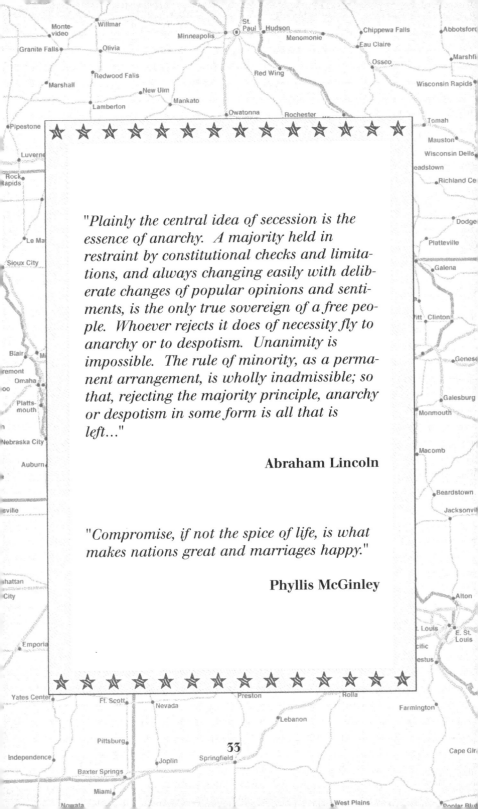

"*Plainly the central idea of secession is the essence of anarchy. A majority held in restraint by constitutional checks and limitations, and always changing easily with deliberate changes of popular opinions and sentiments, is the only true sovereign of a free people. Whoever rejects it does of necessity fly to anarchy or to despotism. Unanimity is impossible. The rule of minority, as a permanent arrangement, is wholly inadmissible; so that, rejecting the majority principle, anarchy or despotism in some form is all that is left...*"

Abraham Lincoln

"*Compromise, if not the spice of life, is what makes nations great and marriages happy.*"

Phyllis McGinley

Nantucket
CRANBERRY SAUCE

4 cups (one pound)
fresh cranberries

2 cups sugar

2 cups water

1/2 cup chopped
walnuts (optional)

Directions:

1. Pour water and sugar into sauce pan.

2. Heat to boiling and then boil for 5 minutes.

3. Add cranberries.

4. Cook for about 5 minutes or until skins pop.

5. Add walnuts if desired.

6. Serve either warm or cold.

★ ★ ★ ★ ★ ★ ★ ★ ★ ★ ★ ★ ★ ★ ★ ★

"When I say I believe in a square deal I do not mean…to give every man the best hand. If the cards do not come to any man, or if they do come, and he has not got the power to play them, that is his affair. All I mean is that there shall be no crookedness in the dealing."

Theodore Roosevelt
1905

"But once war is forced upon us, there is no other alternative than to apply every available means to bring it to a swift end. War's very object is victory-not prolonged indecision….
In war, indeed, there can be no substitute for victory."

General Douglas MacArthur
April 11, 1951

★ ★ ★ ★ ★ ★ ★ ★ ★ ★ ★ ★ ★ ★ ★ ★

Hamilton's
HOMEMADE BREAD

1/4 cup warm water

6 cups flour

1 tablespoon yeast

1/6 cup sugar

1-1/2 tablespoon salt

1/6 cup oil

2-1/2 cups water

Directions:

1. Combine yeast, 1 teaspoon of sugar, and 1/4 cup lukewarm water.
2. In separate bowl, pour flour, sugar, and salt and make indentation or "well".
3. Pour water and yeast mixture into well.
4. Stir until too stiff to stir, then add oil.
5. Knead dough until well-blended.
6. Cover, place in warm place and allow rise, then punch down and allow to rise again.
7. Place dough into 2 loaf pans and allow to rise.
8. Bake at 350 degrees for 35-40 minutes.

"*It is logical that the United States should do whatever it is able to do to assist in the return of normal economic health in the world, without which there can be no political stability and no assured peace. Our policy is directed not against any country or doctrine but against hunger, poverty, desperation, and chaos.*"

George C. Marshall
June 5, 1947

"*Education makes a people easy to lead, but difficult to drive; easy to govern but impossible to enslave.*"

Lord Brougham

Baseball Park
HOT DOG BUNS

2 eggs	2 tablespoons yeast
7-8 cups flour	2 cups water
3/4 cup shortening	1 tablespoon salt

Instructions:

1. Add yeast to warm water with 1 teaspoon of sugar and set aside.

2. In separate bowl, mix shortening, 4 cups flour, sugar, salt and eggs.

3. Beat until smooth, then add yeast mixture and mix thoroughly.

4. Stir in enough of the remaining flour to make a soft dough.

5. Knead on floured board until smooth, then place in greased bowl in warm area and cover with cloth.

6. Allow to rise to double it's size. Punch down, then divide in half.

7. Divide each half into 12 portions and shape them into hot-dog bun shaped fingers roughly 1/2 inch wide.

8. Place on greased baking tin, cover, and let rise until roughly double in size.

9. Bake at 375 degrees for 10 minutes, then brush with butter.

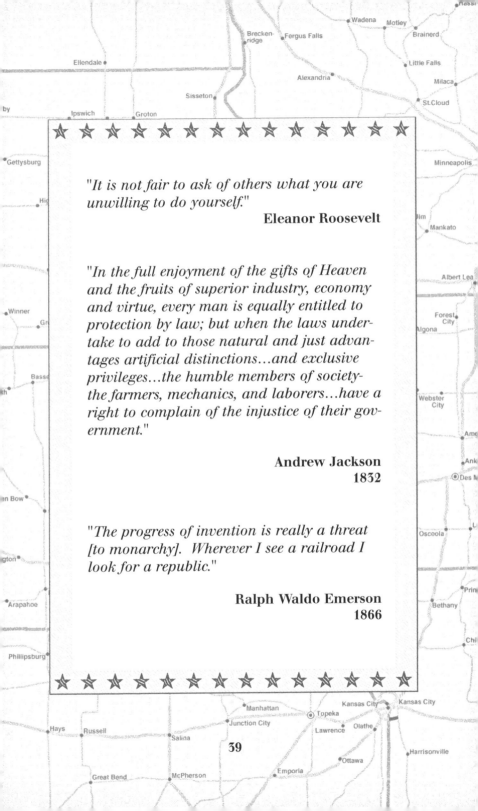

"*It is not fair to ask of others what you are unwilling to do yourself.*"

Eleanor Roosevelt

"*In the full enjoyment of the gifts of Heaven and the fruits of superior industry, economy and virtue, every man is equally entitled to protection by law; but when the laws undertake to add to those natural and just advantages artificial distinctions...and exclusive privileges...the humble members of society- the farmers, mechanics, and laborers...have a right to complain of the injustice of their government.*"

Andrew Jackson
1832

"*The progress of invention is really a threat [to monarchy]. Wherever I see a railroad I look for a republic.*"

Ralph Waldo Emerson
1866

Cony Island
PICKLE RELISH

24 large cucumbers

8 large onions

8 green peppers

6 red peppers

2 quarts white vinegar

8 teaspoons mustard seed

8 teaspoons celery seed

6 teaspoons turmeric

9 cups sugar

4 teaspoons salt

1 teaspoon cloves

Instructions:

1. Grind the cucumbers, onions, and peppers and boil in 2-quarts water for 15 minutes.
2. Drain using cheese cloth or large flour sack.
3. Mix with the remaining ingredients; bring to a boil for 5 minutes.
4. Pour into sterilized hot jars and seal.

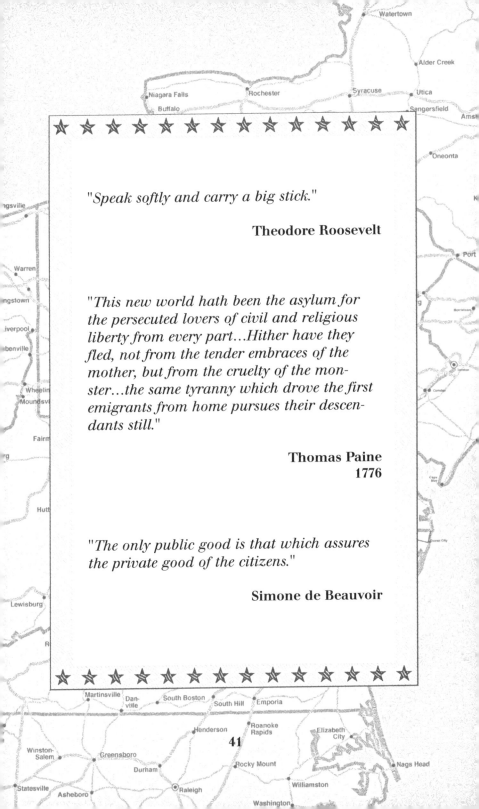

"Speak softly and carry a big stick."

Theodore Roosevelt

"This new world hath been the asylum for the persecuted lovers of civil and religious liberty from every part...Hither have they fled, not from the tender embraces of the mother, but from the cruelty of the monster...the same tyranny which drove the first emigrants from home pursues their descendants still."

Thomas Paine
1776

"The only public good is that which assures the private good of the citizens."

Simone de Beauvoir

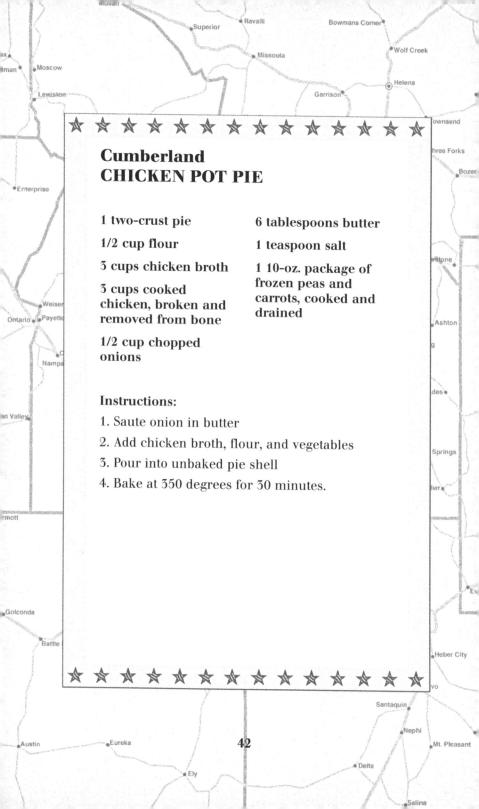

Cumberland
CHICKEN POT PIE

1 two-crust pie

1/2 cup flour

3 cups chicken broth

3 cups cooked chicken, broken and removed from bone

1/2 cup chopped onions

6 tablespoons butter

1 teaspoon salt

1 10-oz. package of frozen peas and carrots, cooked and drained

Instructions:

1. Saute onion in butter
2. Add chicken broth, flour, and vegetables
3. Pour into unbaked pie shell
4. Bake at 350 degrees for 30 minutes.

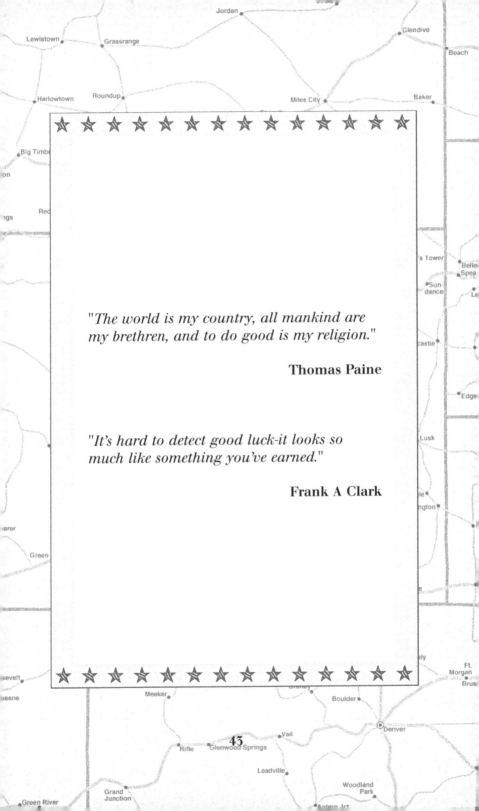

"*The world is my country, all mankind are my brethren, and to do good is my religion.*"

Thomas Paine

"*It's hard to detect good luck-it looks so much like something you've earned.*"

Frank A Clark

Old North Church
CHICKEN AND DUMPLINGS

1 stewed chicken	1/2 teaspoon salt
1 cup wheat flour	2 tablespoons diced onions
2 teaspoons baking powder	1-1/4 cup water
1/2 cup milk	1 small can mushrooms
2 tablespoons salad oil	1 can cream of chicken soup

Instructions:

1. Place chicken in large pot or kettle with enough water to completely cover.

2. Add 2 tablespoons chopped onions.

3. Cover pan and bring to a low boil at low heat for 2-1/2 hours or until tender.

4. Mix flour, baking soda, and salt.

5. Add milk, and oil to dry ingredients and stir just enough to mix.

6. Using tablespoon, drop spoonfuls of dough into boiling pot on top of chicken. Do not allow batter to drop directly into water.

7. Cover tightly again and allow to simmer for 12-15 minutes.

8. Remove dumplings and chicken to hot platter; keep hot while preparing gravy.

9. When gravy is ready, pour over chicken and dumplings.

★ ★ ★ ★ ★ ★ ★ ★ ★ ★ ★ ★ ★ ★ ★

"To get profit without risk, experience without danger, and reward without work is as impossible as it is to live without being born."

A.P. Gourley

"Though passion may have strained it must not break our bonds of affection. The mystic chords of memory, stretching from every battlefield and patriot grave to every living heart and hearthstone all over this broad land, will yet swell the chorus of the Union, when again touched, as surely they will be, by the better angels of our nature."

Abraham Lincoln
1861

★ ★ ★ ★ ★ ★ ★ ★ ★ ★ ★ ★ ★ ★ ★

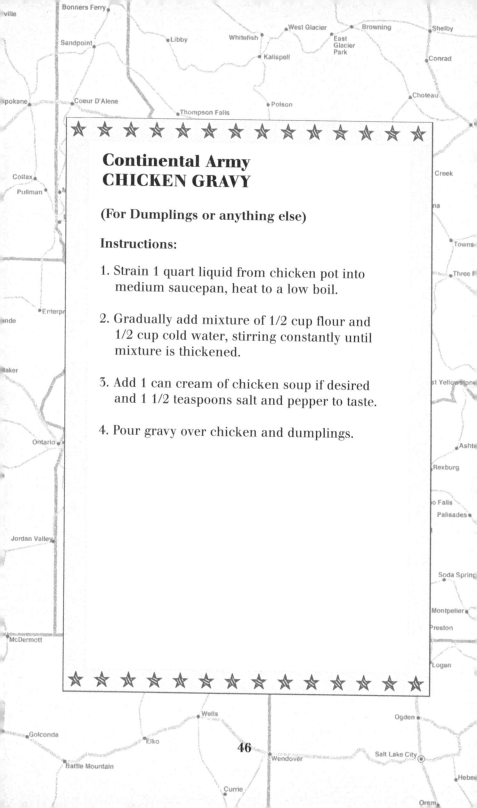

Continental Army
CHICKEN GRAVY

(For Dumplings or anything else)

Instructions:

1. Strain 1 quart liquid from chicken pot into medium saucepan, heat to a low boil.

2. Gradually add mixture of 1/2 cup flour and 1/2 cup cold water, stirring constantly until mixture is thickened.

3. Add 1 can cream of chicken soup if desired and 1 1/2 teaspoons salt and pepper to taste.

4. Pour gravy over chicken and dumplings.

★ ★ ★ ★ ★ ★ ★ ★ ★ ★ ★ ★ ★ ★

"Would you live with ease, then do as you ought, and not as you please."

Benjamin Franklin

"The American continents...are henceforth not to be considered as subjects for future colonization by any European powers."

James Monroe
December 2, 1823

"We conclude that in the field of public education the doctrine of "separate but equal" has no place. Separate educational facilities are inherently unequal."

U.S. Supreme Court
October 1953

★ ★ ★ ★ ★ ★ ★ ★ ★ ★ ★ ★ ★ ★

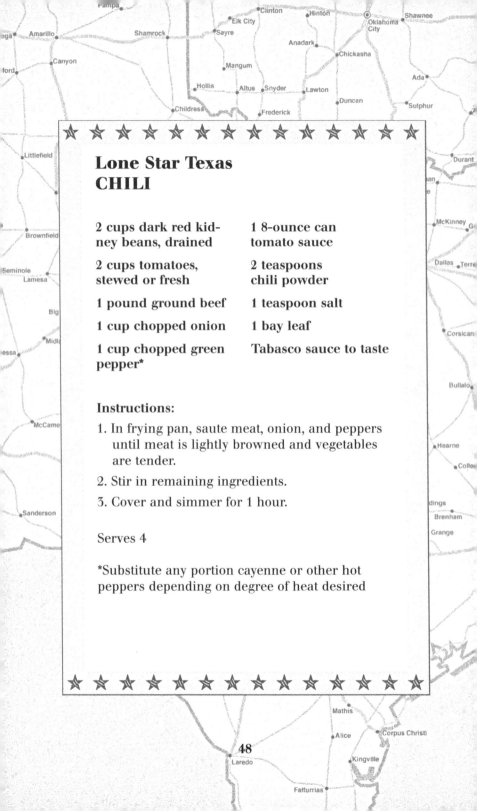

Lone Star Texas
CHILI

2 cups dark red kidney beans, drained

1 8-ounce can tomato sauce

2 cups tomatoes, stewed or fresh

2 teaspoons chili powder

1 pound ground beef

1 teaspoon salt

1 cup chopped onion

1 bay leaf

1 cup chopped green pepper*

Tabasco sauce to taste

Instructions:

1. In frying pan, saute meat, onion, and peppers until meat is lightly browned and vegetables are tender.

2. Stir in remaining ingredients.

3. Cover and simmer for 1 hour.

Serves 4

*Substitute any portion cayenne or other hot peppers depending on degree of heat desired

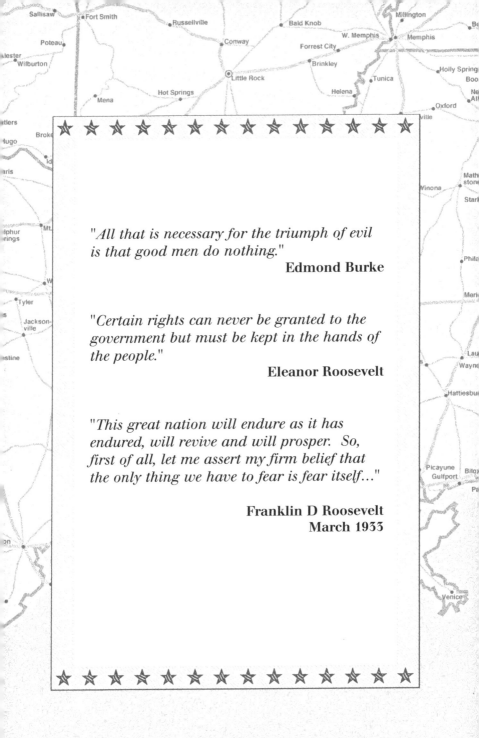

"*All that is necessary for the triumph of evil is that good men do nothing.*"

Edmond Burke

"*Certain rights can never be granted to the government but must be kept in the hands of the people.*"

Eleanor Roosevelt

"*This great nation will endure as it has endured, will revive and will prosper. So, first of all, let me assert my firm belief that the only thing we have to fear is fear itself...*"

Franklin D Roosevelt
March 1933

Alaskan
CRAB STUFFED POTATOES

4 medium Idaho
Potatoes, Scrubbed
clean

1/2 cup butter

1/2 cup half and
half

1 teaspoon salt

4 teaspoons finely
chopped scallions,
green tops included

1 cup grated
Monterey Jack
cheese

1/2 pound fresh
crab meat, cleaned
Paprika for color

Bake potatoes. Cut in half, and scoop out insides. Thoroughly mash potatoes with butter, cream, salt, pepper, onion and cheese. Cool slightly. Fold in crab meat and refill shells. Sprinkle with paprika. Potatoes may then be wrapped in foil and frozen if desired. Thaw, if frozen, and bake at 350 for 20 to 30 minutes.

Nantucket
SHRIMP SKORPIOS

5 tablespoons olive oil

4 cups chopped onions

1 1/2 tablespoons dry mustard

6 tablespoons fresh dill (or 3 tablespoons dried)

1 tablespoon sugar

salt and freshly ground pepper to taste

1 1/2 (35 ounces) cans Italian plum tomatoes

2 pounds headless raw shrimp, shelled and deveined

1/2 pound feta cheese

Heat olive oil in a large pot. Add onions, mustard, dill, sugar, salt and pepper. Saute, stirring, until onions are tender. Add tomatoes and mash them down with a potato masher or wooden spoon. Over medium heat, cook gently 20 minutes (uncovered), or until most of the liquid has evaporated, stirring occasionally. In a casserole, combine shrimp and sauce. Crumble cheese and sprinkle on top. Bake at 350 for 20 minutes or until shrimp are pink.

South-West SALSA

2 quarts tomatoes

**1 green pepper,
chopped**

**1 large onion,
chopped**

1 tablespoon vinegar

1 teaspoon sugar

Instructions:

1. Combine ingredients in a large saucepan and simmer for 45 minutes.

2. Add hot peppers or Tabasco to taste.

3. Serve with grated cheese on top.

"Men are equal; it is not birth but virtue that makes the difference."

Voltaire

"The benign parent of the Human Race...has been pleased to favor the American people with opportunities for deliberating in perfect tranquility, and dispositions for deciding in unparalleled unanimity on a form of government for the security of their union and advancement of their happiness."

George Washington

"The progression of emancipation of any class usually, if not always, takes place through the efforts of individuals of that class."

Harriet Martineau

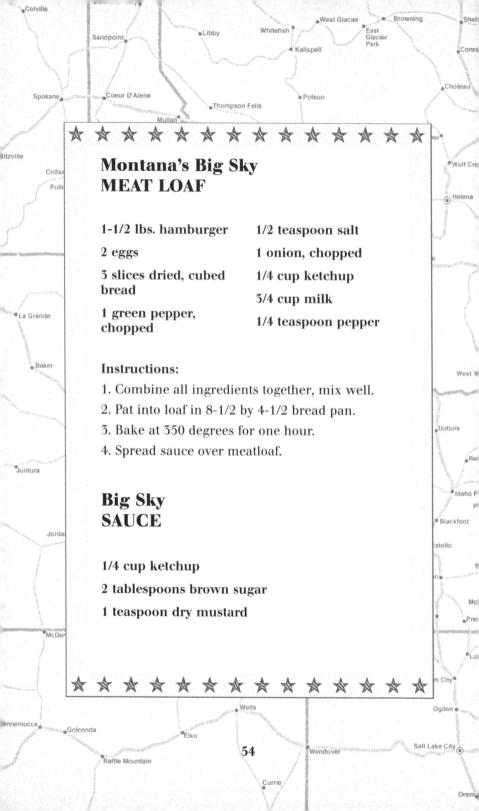

Montana's Big Sky
MEAT LOAF

1-1/2 lbs. hamburger	1/2 teaspoon salt
2 eggs	1 onion, chopped
3 slices dried, cubed bread	1/4 cup ketchup
	3/4 cup milk
1 green pepper, chopped	1/4 teaspoon pepper

Instructions:

1. Combine all ingredients together, mix well.
2. Pat into loaf in 8-1/2 by 4-1/2 bread pan.
3. Bake at 350 degrees for one hour.
4. Spread sauce over meatloaf.

Big Sky
SAUCE

1/4 cup ketchup

2 tablespoons brown sugar

1 teaspoon dry mustard

✮ ✮ ✮ ✮ ✮ ✮ ✮ ✮ ✮ ✮ ✮ ✮ ✮ ✮

"Intellectuals are people who believe that ideas are of more importance than values. That is to say, their own ideas and other people's values."

Gerald Brenan

"Deeds, not stones, are the true monuments of the great."

John L. Motley

"With malice toward none, with charity for all, with firmness in the right as God gives us to see the right, let us strive on to finish the work we are in, to bind up the nations wounds, to care for him who shall have borne the battle and for his widow and orphan, to do all which may achieve and cherish a just and lasting peace among ourselves and with all nations."

Abraham Lincoln

✮ ✮ ✮ ✮ ✮ ✮ ✮ ✮ ✮ ✮ ✮ ✮ ✮ ✮

Idaho
BIG POTATO CASSEROLE

8 medium potatoes

2 cans cream of chicken soup

1 cup sour cream

1/2 cup grated cheese

2 oz. butter or margarine, melted

1/2 cup diced onion

2 cups crushed corn flakes

2 tablespoons melted butter

Instructions:

1. Boil potatoes until soft.

2. Cool and grate potatoes.

3. Mix all ingredients except corn flakes and 2 tablespoons butter.

4. Stir in potatoes.

5. Mix well and place in buttered casserole dish.

6. Top with corn flakes moistened with melted butter.

7. Bake at 350 degrees for 30 minutes.

"As our case is new, so we must think anew and act anew. We must disenthrall ourselves, and then we shall save our country."

Abraham Lincoln
1862

"In these days, it is doubtful that any child may reasonably be expected to succeed in life if he is denied the opportunity of an education. Such an opportunity, where the state has undertaken to provide it, is a right which must be made available to all on equal terms."

Chief Justice Thurgood Marshall

"A perpetual holiday is a good definition of Hell"

George Bernard Shaw

Old West
SHEPHERDS' PIE

1-1/2 lbs. lean ground beef

1 can cream of mushroom soup

2 cups mashed potatoes

1 egg

2 tablespoons salad oil

1 onion (chopped)

1/3 cup celery (chopped)

4 cups sliced mixed vegetables (frozen or fresh)

1/4 teaspoon salt

1/8 teaspoon pepper

Instructions:

1. Brown ground beef and drain off fat
2. Add all other ingredients except egg and mashed potatoes.
3. Heat until mixture comes to boil.
4. Pour mixture into 1-1/2 quart casserole pan or bowl.
5. Mix mashed potatoes with egg and spread mixture over top of casserole.
6. Bake for 30 minutes at 350 degrees or until potatoes are lightly browned.

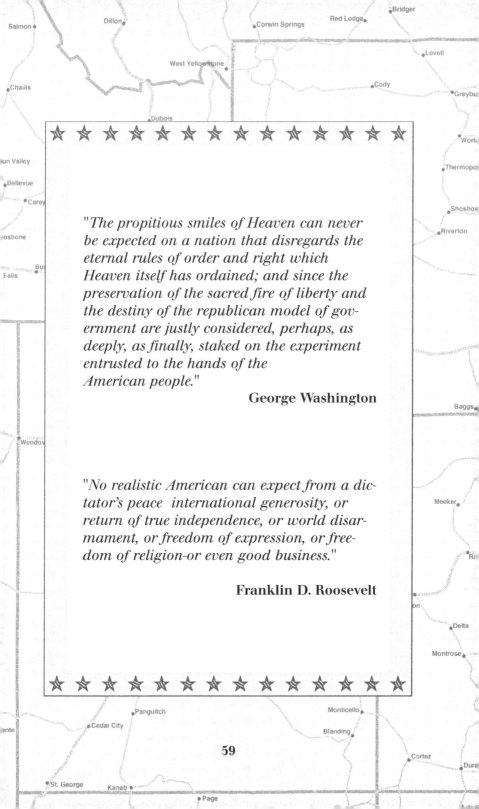

"*The propitious smiles of Heaven can never be expected on a nation that disregards the eternal rules of order and right which Heaven itself has ordained; and since the preservation of the sacred fire of liberty and the destiny of the republican model of government are justly considered, perhaps, as deeply, as finally, staked on the experiment entrusted to the hands of the American people.*"

George Washington

"*No realistic American can expect from a dictator's peace international generosity, or return of true independence, or world disarmament, or freedom of expression, or freedom of religion-or even good business.*"

Franklin D. Roosevelt

Boston Chowder Head
CLAM CHOWDER

7 ounces
minced clams

1/4 cup milk

1/4 cup chopped
bacon

1/2 minced onion

1 10-1/2 ounce can
condensed cream of
potato soup

1 tablespoon vinegar

1/8 teaspoon pepper

Instructions:

1. Cook bacon and onion together in sauce pan until bacon is crisp.

2. Stir in milk and soup stirring occasionally until thoroughly heated.

3. Stir in remaining ingredients until thoroughly heated.

Makes 4 1-cup servings

"The actions of men are the best interpreters of their thoughts."

John Locke

'Driven from every other corner of the earth, freedom of thought and the right of private judgment in matters of conscience direct their course to this happy country as their last asylum."

Samuel Adams

"Two roads diverged in a wood, and I took the one less traveled by, and that has made all the difference."

Robert Frost

Contented Cowboy
GOULASH

1-1/2 pounds lean
ground beef

1 large onion
(chopped)

11 ounces (approx. 1/2
bag) elbow macaroni

1 pint stewed
tomatoes

1 teaspoon
chili powder

1 cup grated
mozzarella cheese

1/4 teaspoon salt

1/8 teaspoon pepper

Instructions:

1. Brown ground beef, chili powder, and
   chopped onion in skillet.

2. Cook macaroni noodles in water (lightly salted
   if desired) until tender.

3. Drain macaroni.

4. Combine all ingredients except cheese in pan
   and simmer for 15 minutes.

5. Sprinkle grated cheese over top and serve.

"Excessive bail shall not be required, no excessive fines imposed, nor cruel and unusual punishments inflicted."

The Bill of Rights

"Any government which maneuvers to block the recovery of other countries cannot expect help from us. Furthermore, governments, political parties, or groups which seek to perpetuate human misery in order to profit there from politically or otherwise will encounter the opposition of the United States."

George C. Marshall

"Destiny is no matter of chance. It is a matter of choice: It is not a thing to be waited for, it is a thing to be achieved."

William Jennings Bryan

63

Original American
NAVAJO FRY BREAD

4 cups flour

1/2 cup powdered milk

1-1/2 teaspoons baking powder

1-1/2 cups warm water

1/2 to 1 cup vegetable oil or melted shortening

Instructions:

1. Heat 1/2 cup oil in frying pan

2. Combine all other ingredients and knead or stir until dough is not sticky. (Add more flour if necessary.)

3. Mold dough with hands and stretch into small, flat pieces (approximately 6 inches by 1/4 inch) and place in hot oil.

4. When dough has bubbled, turn in pan and brown other side.

5. Serve with butter and jam or honey.

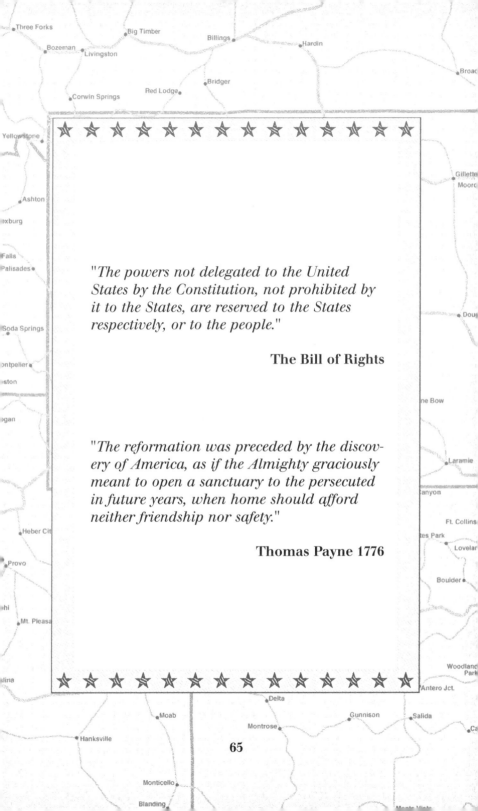

"The powers not delegated to the United States by the Constitution, not prohibited by it to the States, are reserved to the States respectively, or to the people."

The Bill of Rights

"The reformation was preceded by the discovery of America, as if the Almighty graciously meant to open a sanctuary to the persecuted in future years, when home should afford neither friendship nor safety."

Thomas Payne 1776

Aunt Polly's Homemade CHICKEN SOUP

2 to 3 pound boiled chicken

1 tablespoon chopped onion

1-1/2 cups noodles

1 bay leaf

1/2 teaspoon salt

1/8 teaspoon pepper

Instructions:

1. Place chicken, salt and pepper in pot and cover with water.
2. Heat to boiling and simmer until chicken is tender (about 1-1/2 hours)
3. Remove chicken from pot, remove chicken meat from bones and cut into small pieces.
4. Pour broth into medium sauce pan, then add remaining ingredients and chicken meat.
5. Boil until noodles are tender (10-15 minutes).

Makes 6 servings

" *Our mission is at once the oldest and the most basic of this country: to right wrong, to do justice, to serve man....*"

Lindon B. Johnson
1965

"*A well regulated militia, being necessary to the security of a free state, the right of the people to keep and bear arms shall not be infringed.*"

**The Second Amendment
to the Constitution of the United States**

67

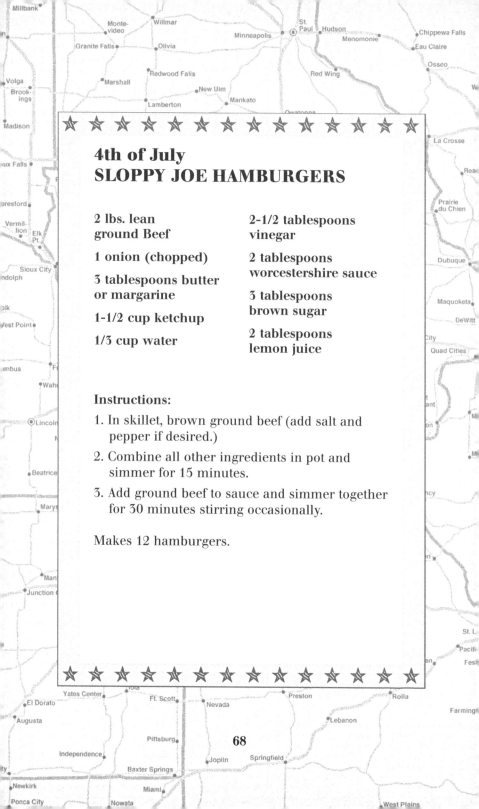

4th of July
SLOPPY JOE HAMBURGERS

2 lbs. lean
ground Beef

1 onion (chopped)

3 tablespoons butter
or margarine

1-1/2 cup ketchup

1/3 cup water

2-1/2 tablespoons
vinegar

2 tablespoons
worcestershire sauce

3 tablespoons
brown sugar

2 tablespoons
lemon juice

Instructions:

1. In skillet, brown ground beef (add salt and
   pepper if desired.)
2. Combine all other ingredients in pot and
   simmer for 15 minutes.
3. Add ground beef to sauce and simmer together
   for 30 minutes stirring occasionally.

Makes 12 hamburgers.

"Today [a] new world is struggling to be born, a world quite different from the one we've known, a world where the rule of law supplants the rule of the jungle, a world where nations recognize the shared responsibility for freedom and justice, a world where the strong respect the rights of the weak...how we manage this crisis today could shape the future for generations to come.... if we do not continue to demonstrate our determination, it would be a signal to actual and potential despots around the world. America and the world must defend common vital interests – and we will. America and the world must support the rule of law – and we will. America and the world must stand up to aggression-and we will. And one thing more: in pursuit of these goals America will not be intimidated."

George Bush
1990

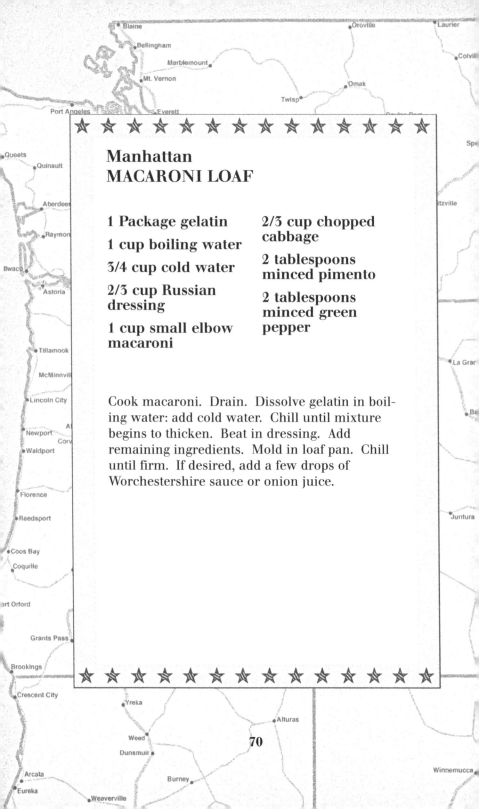

Manhattan
MACARONI LOAF

1 Package gelatin

1 cup boiling water

3/4 cup cold water

2/3 cup Russian dressing

1 cup small elbow macaroni

2/3 cup chopped cabbage

2 tablespoons minced pimento

2 tablespoons minced green pepper

Cook macaroni. Drain. Dissolve gelatin in boiling water: add cold water. Chill until mixture begins to thicken. Beat in dressing. Add remaining ingredients. Mold in loaf pan. Chill until firm. If desired, add a few drops of Worchestershire sauce or onion juice.

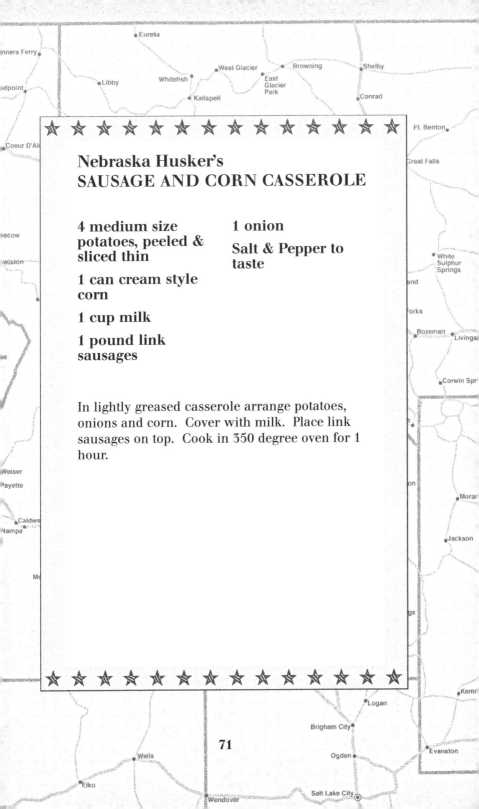

Nebraska Husker's
SAUSAGE AND CORN CASSEROLE

4 medium size potatoes, peeled & sliced thin

1 can cream style corn

1 cup milk

1 pound link sausages

1 onion

Salt & Pepper to taste

In lightly greased casserole arrange potatoes, onions and corn. Cover with milk. Place link sausages on top. Cook in 350 degree oven for 1 hour.

Oklahoma
RANCH HAND STEW

3-1/2 lbs. beef cut into cubes

2 large potatoes sliced into 1 inch cubes

3 large carrots, sliced

4 onions, chopped

2 Tablespoons flour

2 Tablespoons butter or salad oil

1 1/2 cup water

1 teaspoon chili powder (optional)

Salt and pepper to taste

(May also add nearly any vegetable you have on hand if desired.)

Instructions:

1. Dust meat cubes with flour and brown in buttered or oiled pan.

2. Add water, cover, and simmer over low heat for about two hours.

3. Add potatoes and carrots at about 1 hour and other vegetables with 15 minutes remaining or cook until tender.

"Men cannot for long live hopefully unless they are embarked upon some great unifying enterprise, one for which they may pledge their lives, their fortunes, and their honor."

C.A. Dykstra

"Congress shall make no law respecting an establishment of religion, or prohibiting the free exercise thereof; or abridging the freedom of speech, or of the press; or the right of the people peaceably to assemble, and to petition the Government for a redress of grievances."

**The First Amendment
to the Constitution of The United States**

75

49er Sourdough MUFFINS

1/2 cup sourdough	1/2 cup brown sugar
2 cups flour	1 cup raisins
2 eggs	1 teaspoon soda
1/2 cup shortening, melted	1 teaspoon salt
1/2 cup undiluted canned, evaporated milk	

Instructions:

1. Combine all ingredients stirring only enough to blend.
2. Pre-heat oven to 425 degrees.
3. Bake in greased muffin pan for 25 minutes or until lightly browned on top.

"We have no selfish ends to serve. We desire no conquest, no dominion. We seek no indemnities for ourselves, no material compensation for the sacrifices we shall freely make. We are but one of the champions of the rights of mankind. We shall be satisfied when those rights have been made as secure as the faith and freedom of nations can make them..."

Woodrow Wilson
1917

"The only failure a man ought to fear is failure in cleaving to the purpose he sees to be best."

George Eliot

EGGS BENEDICT
Arnold

4 hard-boiled eggs

1/4 cup butter or margarine

3 tablespoons flour

1/4 teaspoon salt

1/8 teaspoon pepper

2 1/2 cups milk

1/2 loaf sliced toast

Instructions:

Step 1:

1. Hard boil 4 eggs.
2. Cool and peel.
3. Dice whites.
4. Grate yolks in separate bowl.

Step 2:

1. Melt butter in sauce pan.
2. Stir in flour, salt and pepper.
3. Slowly add milk stirring constantly over low heat until thick.
4. Stir in chopped egg whites and serve on top of toast.
5. Sprinkle with grated egg yolks.

✦ ✦ ✦ ✦ ✦ ✦ ✦ ✦ ✦ ✦ ✦ ✦ ✦ ✦

"One way of life is based upon the will of the majority, and is distinguished by free institutions, representative government, free elections, guarantees of individual liberty, freedom of speech and religion, and freedom from political oppression.

The second way of life is based upon the will of a minority forcibly imposed upon the majority. It relies upon terror and oppression, a controlled press and radio, fixed elections, and the suppression of personal freedoms.

I believe that it must be the policy of the United States to support free people who are resisting attempted subjugation by armed minorities or by outside pressures."

Harry S. Truman
March 12, 1947

✦ ✦ ✦ ✦ ✦ ✦ ✦ ✦ ✦ ✦ ✦ ✦ ✦ ✦

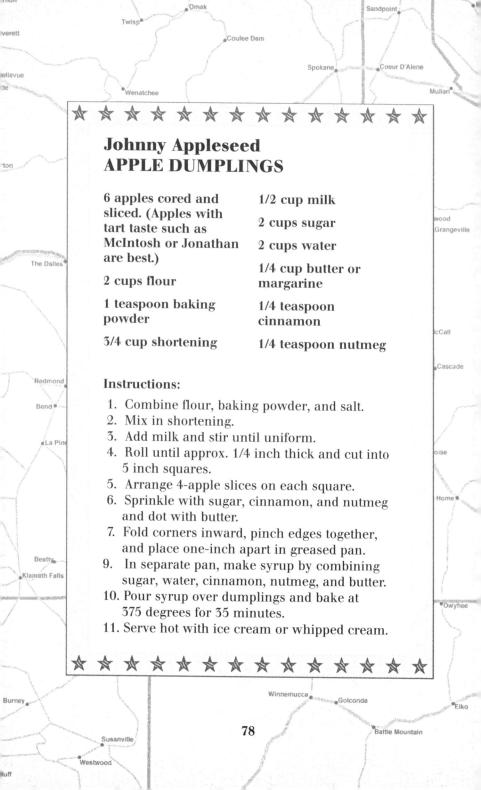

Johnny Appleseed
APPLE DUMPLINGS

6 apples cored and sliced. (Apples with tart taste such as McIntosh or Jonathan are best.)

2 cups flour

1 teaspoon baking powder

3/4 cup shortening

1/2 cup milk

2 cups sugar

2 cups water

1/4 cup butter or margarine

1/4 teaspoon cinnamon

1/4 teaspoon nutmeg

Instructions:

1. Combine flour, baking powder, and salt.
2. Mix in shortening.
3. Add milk and stir until uniform.
4. Roll until approx. 1/4 inch thick and cut into 5 inch squares.
5. Arrange 4-apple slices on each square.
6. Sprinkle with sugar, cinnamon, and nutmeg and dot with butter.
7. Fold corners inward, pinch edges together, and place one-inch apart in greased pan.
9. In separate pan, make syrup by combining sugar, water, cinnamon, nutmeg, and butter.
10. Pour syrup over dumplings and bake at 375 degrees for 35 minutes.
11. Serve hot with ice cream or whipped cream.

"Not all the treasures of the world, so far as I believe, could have induced me to support an offensive war."

Thomas Payne

"The right of citizens of the United States to vote shall not be denied or abridged by the United States or by any State on account of sex."

The 19th Amendment to the Constitution of the United States

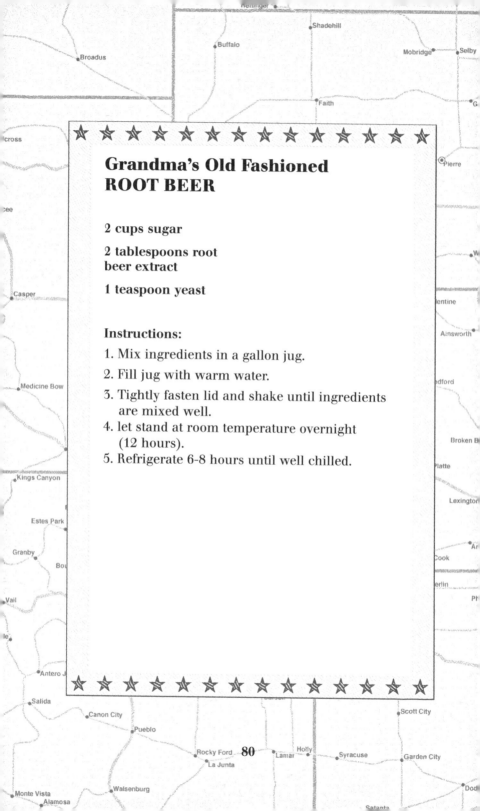

Grandma's Old Fashioned
ROOT BEER

2 cups sugar

2 tablespoons root beer extract

1 teaspoon yeast

Instructions:

1. Mix ingredients in a gallon jug.
2. Fill jug with warm water.
3. Tightly fasten lid and shake until ingredients are mixed well.
4. let stand at room temperature overnight (12 hours).
5. Refrigerate 6-8 hours until well chilled.

"When I was first honored with a call into the service of my country, then on the eve of an arduous struggle for its liberties, the light in which I contemplated my duty required that I should renounce every pecuniary compensation."

George Washington

"Great minds have purposes, others have wishes."

Washington Irving

Boston Tea Party
SUGAR COOKIES

3-1/2 cups flour (sifted)

1 cup sugar

1/2 cup shortening

1 egg (beaten)

1/2 cup thick sour cream

1 teaspoon vanilla

1/2 teaspoon salt

1 teaspoon soda

Instructions:

1. Sift flour, soda, and salt together in a bowl.

2. Beat sugar, shortening, egg, and vanilla for 2 minutes, scraping bowl while beating.

3. Add flour mixture and sour cream and continue beating for another 1-1/2 minutes.

4. Roll out on lightly floured surface until 1/4 inch thick.

5. Cut cookies, sprinkle with sugar, and bake on greased cookie sheet for 8-10 minutes or until golden brown.

"Now, I confess myself as belonging to that class in the country who contemplate slavery as a moral, social, and political evil..."

Abraham Lincoln

"...our security is based on being prepared to meet all threats..."

Ronald Reagan

"I am in earnest. I will not equivocate. I will not excuse. I will not retreat a single inch. And I will be heard!"

William Lloyd Garrison

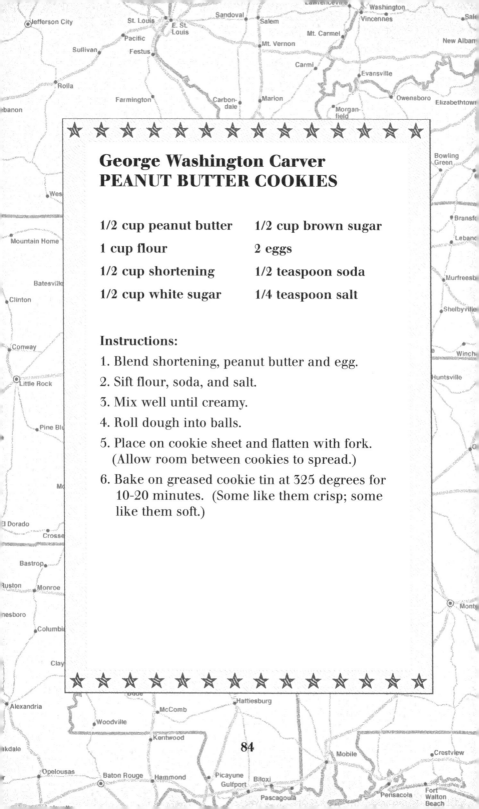

George Washington Carver
PEANUT BUTTER COOKIES

1/2 cup peanut butter	1/2 cup brown sugar
1 cup flour	2 eggs
1/2 cup shortening	1/2 teaspoon soda
1/2 cup white sugar	1/4 teaspoon salt

Instructions:

1. Blend shortening, peanut butter and egg.
2. Sift flour, soda, and salt.
3. Mix well until creamy.
4. Roll dough into balls.
5. Place on cookie sheet and flatten with fork. (Allow room between cookies to spread.)
6. Bake on greased cookie tin at 325 degrees for 10-20 minutes. (Some like them crisp; some like them soft.)

★ ★ ★ ★ ★ ★ ★ ★ ★ ★ ★ ★ ★

"As we peer into society's future, we – you and I, and our government – must avoid the impulse to live only for today, plundering, for our own ease and convenience, the precious resources of tomorrow."

Dwight D. Eisenhower

"Be bold. If you're going to make an error, make a doozy, and don't be afraid to hit the ball."

Billie Jean King

★ ★ ★ ★ ★ ★ ★ ★ ★ ★ ★ ★ ★

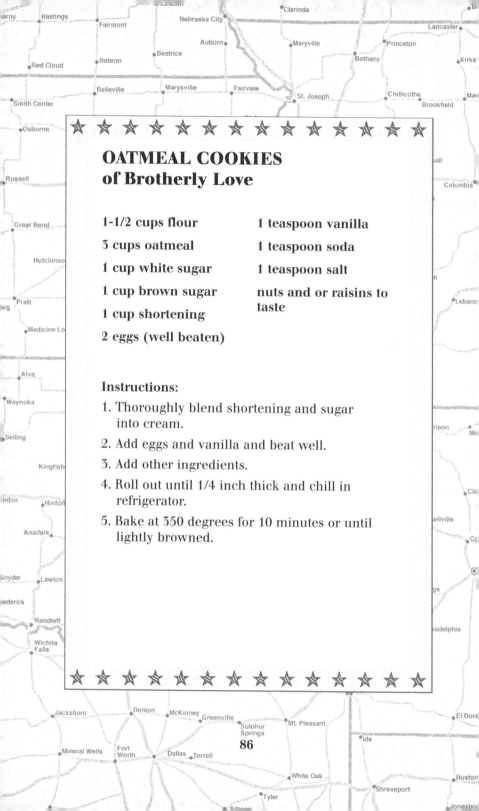

OATMEAL COOKIES
of Brotherly Love

1-1/2 cups flour

3 cups oatmeal

1 cup white sugar

1 cup brown sugar

1 cup shortening

2 eggs (well beaten)

1 teaspoon vanilla

1 teaspoon soda

1 teaspoon salt

nuts and or raisins to taste

Instructions:

1. Thoroughly blend shortening and sugar into cream.
2. Add eggs and vanilla and beat well.
3. Add other ingredients.
4. Roll out until 1/4 inch thick and chill in refrigerator.
5. Bake at 350 degrees for 10 minutes or until lightly browned.

'I behold the surest pledges that…no local prejudices or attachments, no separate views or party animosities, will misdirect the comprehensive and equal eye which ought to watch over this great assemblage of communities and interests."

George Washington
First Inaugural Address - 1789

"In a democracy, the individual enjoys not only the ultimate power but carries the ultimate responsibility."

Norman Cousins

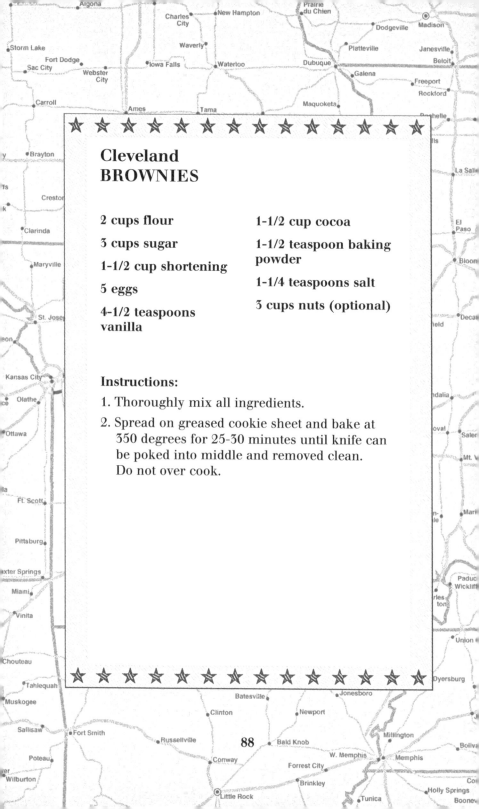

Cleveland
BROWNIES

2 cups flour

3 cups sugar

1-1/2 cup shortening

5 eggs

4-1/2 teaspoons vanilla

1-1/2 cup cocoa

1-1/2 teaspoon baking powder

1-1/4 teaspoons salt

3 cups nuts (optional)

Instructions:

1. Thoroughly mix all ingredients.

2. Spread on greased cookie sheet and bake at 350 degrees for 25-30 minutes until knife can be poked into middle and removed clean. Do not over cook.

> *"No person shall be held to answer for a capital, or otherwise infamous crime, unless on a presentment of indictment of a grand jury...nor shall any person be subject for the same offense to be twice put in jeopardy of life or limb; nor shall be compelled in any criminal case to be a witness against himself, nor be deprived of life, liberty, or property, without due process of law; nor shall private property be taken for public use without just compensation."*

**5th amendment
to the Constitution of the United States**

> *"Freedom and tyranny cannot exist in close proximity because tyrants cannot control people who have witnessed freedom."*

Anonymous

Georgia
PEANUT BRITTLE

2 cups sugar

2 cups chopped peanuts (can be salted or plain)

1 cup light corn syrup

1 cup butter or margarine

1 teaspoon soda

1/2 cup water

Instructions:

1. In a 3-quart sauce pan, heat water.

2. Stir in sugar, and syrup until dissolved.

3. While syrup boils, add butter stirring constantly

4. When mixture is 280 degrees, add nuts.

5. When mixture reaches 305 degrees. Remove from heat.

6. Quickly and thoroughly stir in soda.

7. Pour onto 2 cookie sheets and stretch until thin by lifting and pulling from edges with spoons or forks.

8. Loosen from pan as soon as possible and break into pieces.

"…in holding scientific research and discovery in respect as we should, we must also be alert to the…danger that public policy could itself become the captive of a scientific-technological elite.

It is the task of statesmanship to mold, to balance, and to integrate these and other forces, new and old, within the principles of our democratic system-ever aiming toward the supreme goals of our free society."

Dwight D. Eisenhower

"…the right of trial by jury shall be preserved, and no fact tried by a jury shall be otherwise reexamined in any court of the United States, than according to the rules of the common law."

**7th Amendment
to the Constitution of the United States**

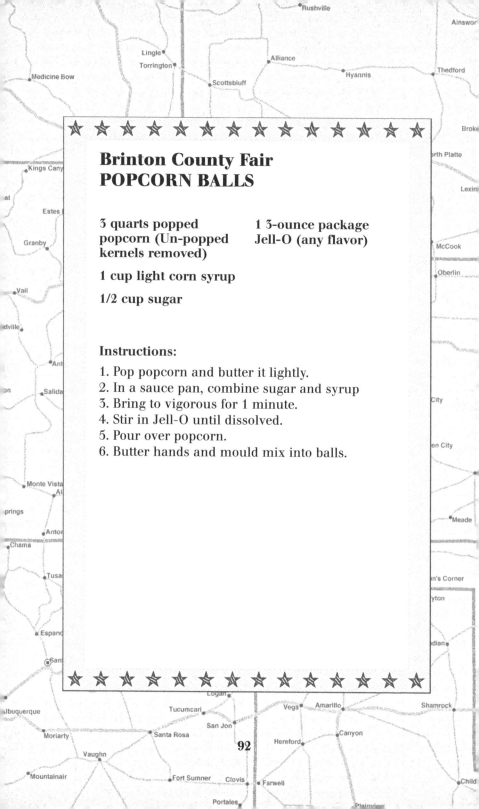

Brinton County Fair
POPCORN BALLS

3 quarts popped
popcorn (Un-popped
kernels removed)

1 3-ounce package
Jell-O (any flavor)

1 cup light corn syrup

1/2 cup sugar

Instructions:

1. Pop popcorn and butter it lightly.
2. In a sauce pan, combine sugar and syrup
3. Bring to vigorous for 1 minute.
4. Stir in Jell-O until dissolved.
5. Pour over popcorn.
6. Butter hands and mould mix into balls.

"If you would be free, you must allow others their freedom."

Anonymous

"...there exists in the economy and course of nature an indissoluble union between virtue and happiness; between duty and advantage..."

George Washington

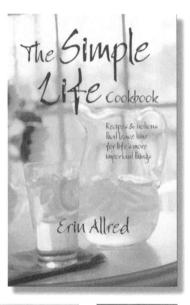

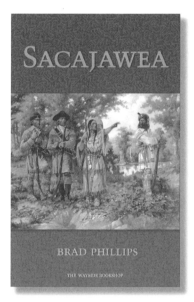

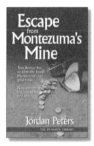

'The Truth About Life' Humor Books

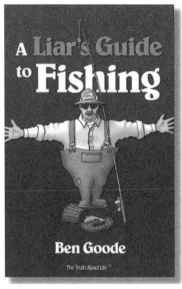

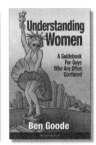

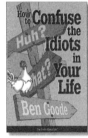

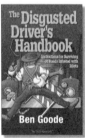

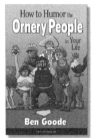

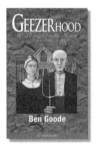

All humor books are $6.95 US.

Apricot Press Order Form

Book Title　　　　　　　　　　**Quantity x Cost / Book = Total**

_____　____　_____　_____

_____　____　_____　_____

_____　____　_____　_____

_____　____　_____　_____

_____　____　_____　_____

_____　____　_____　_____

_____　____　_____　_____

_____　____　_____　_____

Do not send Cash. Mail check or money order to:
**Apricot Press   P.O. Box 1611
American Fork, Utah   84003**
Telephone 801-756-0456
Allow 3 weeks for delivery.

**Quantity discounts available.
Call us for more information.**
9 a.m. - 5 p.m. MST

Sub Total =

Shipping =　**$2.00**

Tax 8.5% =

Total Amount
Enclosed =

Shipping Address

Name:

Street:

City:　　　　　　　　　State:

Zip Code:

Telephone:

Email: